best easy dayhikes
Salt Lake City

Brian Brinkerhoff

FALCON GUIDE®

GUILFORD, CONNECTICUT
HELENA, MONTANA

AN IMPRINT OF THE GLOBE PEQUOT PRESS

A **FALCON** GUIDE ®

Cataloging-in-Publication Data is on record at the Library of Congress.

ISBN-13: 978-1-56044-854-9
ISBN-10: 1-56044-854-7

Manufactured in the United States of America
First Edition/Seventh Printing

To buy books in quantity for corporate use or incentives, call **(800) 962–0973, ext. 4551,** or e-mail **premiums@GlobePequot.com.**

CAUTION

The author and The Globe Pequot Press assume no liability for accidents happening to, or injuries sustained by, readers who engage in the activities described in this book.

This book is dedicated to my wife, Becky,
and my family for their endless love, help, and support,
making this and many other things possible.

Acknowledgments

I am grateful for the help from Tracy Salcedo and George Meyers. Additional thanks to Bob Easton, Tim Garcia, Loyal Clark, and Steve Brown from the USDA Forest Service. I also thank my crew of hiking partners, including Becky, Ron Russon, Jeremy "Harry" Russon, Lanita Evans, Sam Evans, Dallin, Sierra, Sammy, Molina Welcker, Mom, and Dad. Thanks to Eagle/Lowrance Electronics for use of its GPS equipment, which helped generate the maps in this guide. Special thanks to Chris Salcedo, Marlen Madsen, Marc Haddock, Clayton Huber, Val Brinkerhoff, and all others who helped make this book possible.

Contents

Map Legend

Interstate	(00)	Campground	▲
US Highway	(00)	Picnic Area	🛆
State or Other Principal Road	(00) (000)	Cabins/Buildings	■
Forest Road	0000	Peak	9,782 ft.
Interstate Highway	⟹	Bridge	⏝
Paved Road	⟹	Elevation	9,782 ft. ✕
Gravel Road	⟹	Gate	•—•
Unimproved Road	====⟹	Mine Site	⚒
Trailhead	◯	Overlook/Point of Interest	◨
Main Trail	‒‒‒‿‿		
Secondary Trail	‒‒‿‿‒	National Forest/Park Boundary	⌐ ¬ ⌐
Parking Area	(P)	Map Orientation	N
River/Creek	∿		
Marsh	⊻	Scale	0 0.5 1 Miles
One Way Road	One Way		

Salt Lake City

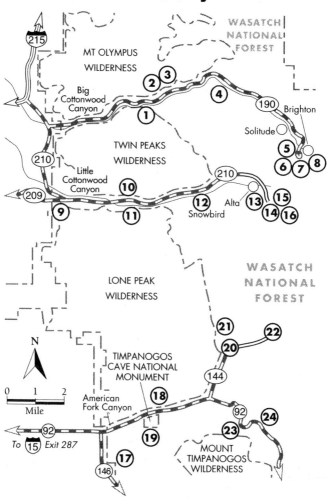

Ranking the Hikes

The following list ranks the hikes in this book from easiest to hardest.

Introduction

What is a "best easy" hike?

Hiking opportunities abound near Salt Lake City, with magnificent adventures awaiting in Big and Little Cottonwood Canyons, and American Fork Canyon. Along with the rich skiing and mining history of these retreats, highlights include sparkling clear streams, tall dark evergreens, and meadows full of wildflowers. These canyons offer adventures for everyone, from journeys for families with youngsters to technical ascents for experienced mountaineers.

This guide focuses on the shorter, easier trails, along with routes suitable for individuals with disabilities. Trails in this guide vary in length and difficulty, although most routes are short and can be covered within a few hours. This guide focuses on hikes in Little Cottonwood Canyon, Big Cottonwood Canyon, and American Fork Canyon, but other opportunities await in surrounding canyons and along the banks of the Jordan River.

You should remember that it's not important to arrive at a destination within a specific time frame, but to enjoy the scenery and travel at a pace comfortable to you. If the trail appears too dangerous or difficult, feel free to stop and return again on another occasion, when conditions are better. The best months to visit these trails usually ranges from late May to October.

To approximate how long it will take you to complete a given trail, use the standard of two miles per hour, adding time if you are not a strong hiker or are traveling with small children, and subtracting time if you are in good shape. Add time for picnics, rest stops or other activities you plan for your outing.

Many of the hikes in this book have been selected because of their relatively short trail lengths, less steep inclines, and unique views. Although listed hikes vary in length and difficulty, all have two key features in common: each is approximately two hours or less in duration and is less than an hour's drive of the canyon mouth in which it is located.

– *Brian Brinkerhoff*

Zero Impact

With the large number of trail users in this state, courtesy has become increasingly important to maintaining positive outdoor experiences for all backcountry visitors. The following suggestions can help make everyone's visit more enjoyable and memorable.

The "Zero Impact" philosophy encompasses a wide range of outdoor ethics, including staying on the trail (to avoid trampling vegetation and increasing erosion), packing out litter, and leaving the environment better looking than when you arrived. The book *Leave No Trace* is a valuable resource for learning more about these principles:

The Falcon Principles of Zero Impact
- *Leave with everything you brought.*
- *Leave no sign of your visit.*
- *Leave the landscape as you found it.*

Unfortunately, less-considerate trail users leave reminders of their visits, including candy wrappers, graffiti, and destruction along the trail. Each item left behind lessens the overall outdoor experience for others. Please pack out all scraps of paper, cans, and packages, including those left by careless individuals. By staying on the trail and following these guidelines, the scenery you came to enjoy will last for many generations.

Avoid taking wildflowers and other souvenirs, including rocks, artifacts from old mines, etc. These items cannot be replaced and when removed lessen the excitement, history, and beauty for others.

Yield to other trail users when appropriate, and be courteous along the way. Many trails are shared by more than one user group, including mountain bikers and horseback riders. These trails can accommodate a wide variety of trail users if all demonstrate a sense of responsibility and respect for others.

In addition, try to avoid making loud noise or playing music along the trail. The mountain tranquility that many seek can be disturbed easily by a single thoughtless visitor.

To minimize impacts on the environment, remember to make pit stops at established outhouse facilities before beginning any hike. If restrooms are unavailable, bury human waste 6 to 8 inches deep and pack out used toilet paper (carry a lightweight trowel for this purpose). Keep waste at least 300 feet from all surface water and marshy areas.

Dogs and horses are not allowed in Big and Little Cottonwood Canyons. These areas are considered watershed for the Salt Lake City area.

Be Prepared

Although hiking can provide numerous rewards, it also can be a dangerous sport, especially for those who come unprepared. Mother Nature should always be given the respect she deserves; a little preparation will go a long way.

In spite of efforts made to alert hikers of potential hazards, not all possible dangers can be covered and you should assume the responsibility for your own actions. Be aware of your surroundings, weather, and physical condition. If something does not appear "right," feel free to head back to the trailhead and return when conditions are better.

Know the basics of first aid, including how to treat bleeding, bites and stings, and fractures, strains or sprains. It is always wise to have a basic first-aid kit on hand, including over-the-counter pain relievers, bandages, and ointments. No matter how short the journey is, a first-aid kit should always be on hand for emergencies.

Bring extra clothing for adverse or cold weather conditions. Although it may feel warm at the trailhead, cold weather can set in unexpectedly, making hypothermia a serious reality. Mountain air temperatures can drop quickly in the evening hours, creating a dangerous scenario. A jacket or sweater will help ward off the cold after the sun sets.

The magnificent sun can make hiking a treat and may illuminate spectacular vistas, but it poses a problem to hikers traveling in the heat of the day. The potential for heat stroke and heat exhaustion can be minimized by wearing a hat and traveling during the cooler, more enjoyable morning and evening hours. A long sleeved shirt and pants will help avoid you sunburn, insect bites, and stinging nettle, which is common along many of the trails. High altitudes can turn relatively short sun exposure into a serious and painful sunburn. Bring plenty of sunscreen and reapply it often to ensure protection from the sun's harmful rays.

Plan plenty of time to complete the journey, including time for resting, relaxing, and enjoying the scenery. For those who hike in the evenings, darkness can make an easy trail difficult to maneuver as it becomes easier to wander off the correct path. Plan enough time to return before darkness sets in. A small flashlight (check the batteries before leaving) is a useful item for your day pack.

Bring plenty of liquids. Even short journeys can result in heat exhaustion or dehydration. Although water may be one of the heaviest items to pack, it is also one of the most important. Bacteria, including *Giardia lamblia*, is present in Wasatch streams, making water undrinkable without a filter or purification tablets (available at most sporting goods stores). It is always wise to bring a full canteen when your path takes you away from water sources.

Bring high-energy snacks for the trail and treats for the youngsters. Little food rewards make the journey seem shorter and provide energy for the trek.

Wear good socks and comfortable walking shoes. To avoid blisters, make sure you wear new shoes around town before using them in the backcountry. Shoes with higher tops provide extra ankle support on rocky slopes.

Let people know where you are going and when you expect to return.

Enjoy the animals you may see along the trail, but keep your distance. The abundance of wildlife is certainly an attraction along the way, but remember that these are wild animals and a safe distance should always be maintained. Some animals (even the cute ones) may bite, spreading pain and disease to the recipient. Watchful and protective mothers usually are not far away from their youngsters, though they may not be visible to the trail user. Don't feed wildlife to avoid disrupting their survival instincts.

Hiking along the Wasatch Front provides spectacular opportunities, but also can host numerous challenges and dangers. Weather can change rapidly, making the trails slick, reducing visibility, and exposing travelers to lightning and other dangerous elements. Keep an eye to the skies for dramatic changes in weather. Clear skies can change within minutes to severe thunderstorms or snowstorms.

A comfortable day pack usually will accommodate all your needs for trails listed in this guide. Be sure to pack rain gear for potential storms, a warm sweater or coat for cooling temperatures, water, food, a first-aid kit, flashlight, and matches.

Additional items that may prove useful on longer hikes, may include a compass and topographical map, a GPS unit, a pocket knife, a whistle to signal for help, and the knowledge of how to use each item properly. You may want to bring a camera with plenty of film, binoculars, and an identification manual for plants and animals you may see along the way.

Big Cottonwood Canyon

Big Cottonwood Canyon is a beautiful and long, bounded by the Mount Olympus Wilderness to the north and the Twin Peaks Wilderness to the south. Steep canyon walls restrict hiking opportunities along the lower stretches, but are popular with rock-climbing enthusiasts. Brighton and Solitude ski areas are celebrated winter destinations for skiers seeking what some believe to be the finest snow in the world. Amidst these features are quiet stands of quaking aspen, tall fragrant evergreen forests, numerous quiet lakes, and miles of hiking opportunities.

Geological and hydrological activity, which created the steep, towering mountains, has made for spectacular viewing, but also has made for steep and strenuous hikes. These hikes were selected for their more gradual inclines and relatively short distances.

Whether you seek a family stroll around the boardwalks of Silver Lake, the silence of Lake Solitude, or the excitement of Donut Falls, Big Cottonwood Canyon can fill your summer with wonderful memories.

To reach Big Cottonwood Canyon, follow the Interstate 215 "belt loop" south (or east if you are coming from the southern and western portions of Salt Lake City) to Exit 7. From the exit, drive southeast on Utah 190. This road takes you to the mouth of Big Cottonwood Canyon, then up the canyon to the Brighton Ski Area. Look for signs pointing to this popular recreation area.

1
MILL B SOUTH
INTERPRETIVE TRAIL

Type of hike: Out-and-back.
Total distance: 0.7 mile.
Elevation gain: 80 feet.
Maps: USGS Mount Aire; USGS Dromedary Peak.
Jurisdiction: Wasatch National Forest.
Finding the trailhead: To reach the trailhead, drive 4.4 miles up Big Cottonwood Canyon on Utah 190. At this point, a small road branches right (southeast) from the lower curve of the "S-Turn" into the trailhead parking lot. A secondary parking area is available before the next curve. This paved interpretive trail heads east and follows Big Cottonwood Creek.

Key points:
0.35 Reach the falls and the end of the paved trail.

The hike: Recently paved to improve accessibility for persons with disabilities, this short trail follows Big Cottonwood Creek to a small waterfall. Rushing water drowns noise from the highway and maintains cooler temperatures along the canyon bottom. A moderate climb for wheelchairs, Forest Service employees hope to place interpretive trail signs along the way, providing improved learning experiences for visitors of all ages.

Mill B South Interpretive Trail

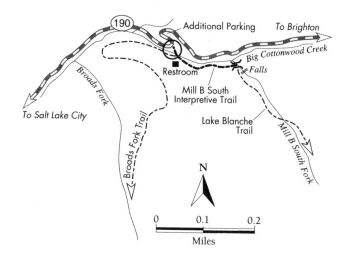

Along this path, you may view several birds, squirrels, or a wary trout in the cold clear waters. Take your time along the way and enjoy the wonders surrounding you. The trail to Lake Blanche branches south from the pavement's end, and another small dirt path can be spotted continuing east, through an abandoned parking area formerly used for the Lake Blanche trailhead. Restoration work is underway to transform this area into a lush green meadow. A small trail leads beyond the clearing and stops near some large boulders along Big Cottonwood Creek.

As you begin up the paved trail, walking east of the restrooms, you will enjoy the sight and sound of cascading water, shaded by cottonwoods and pines. River birch, chokecherry, dogwood, and aster are found along this route.

As you round a bend, you can see rugged cliffs towering ahead. Wild roses, Indian paintbrush, and a variety of yellow flowers also may be spotted, depending on the time of year, while Big Cottonwood Creek roars loudly to your left (north). Abundant shade throughout the day makes this a pleasant journey during the hiking season.

The trail gently climbs above the creek, crossing a bridge to view a small waterfall (0.35 mile). The Lake Blanche Trail begins here, heading to the southeast. You also may take the small dirt path that continues ahead through the abandoned area to the creek, where numerous resting areas await. Return to the trailhead on the same path.

Option: Continue up the Lake Blanche Trail for 2.75 miles to Lake Blanche.

2
HIDDEN FALLS TRAIL

Type of hike: Out-and-back.
Total distance: 0.3 mile.
Elevation gain: 40 feet.
Maps: USGS Mount Aire.
Jurisdiction: Wasatch National Forest.
Finding the trailhead: To reach the trailhead, drive 4.4 miles up Big Cottonwood Canyon on Utah 190. Park in the small lot located on the right (southeast) side of the road in the second, upper curve of the "S-Turn." The trail is on the opposite (north) side of the road. Additional parking and restroom facilities can be found at the lower parking area, where a small road branches right (southeast) from the lower curve of the "S-Turn."

Key points:
0.15 Reach Hidden Falls.

The hike: One of the nicest aspects of Hidden Falls is the short distance required to reach the cooling mist of this secluded retreat. The falling water and hidden location gives one the sense of being far from the road. Tucked away from view of the highway, Hidden Falls is a nice hike for younger children and the elderly. This unpaved route, one of the shortest in this book, takes only minutes to cover, but pro-

Hidden Falls Trail,
Mill B North Fork Trail to Overlook

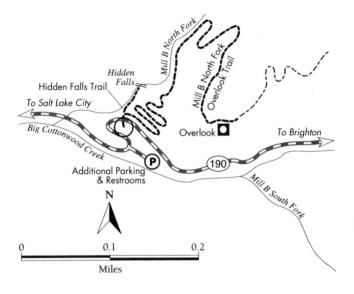

vides terrain interesting enough to make it challenging for youngsters.

An old mine near the falls area adds a sense of mystery to your destination and can be a fun place to share some local history or ghost stories. The mine is gated for everyone's safety, and you are asked to avoid the temptation to try to get inside. Rock climbers also enjoy the area and you may watch them as they scale the surrounding walls.

To begin your journey, head up the stairs near the information signs of the upper parking area, and cross the busy highway, looking both ways before crossing. Keep a close eye on your children.

Take the lower left trail to the falls, heading into the shade of maples and cottonwoods. Avoid the second set of stairs to the right, which continues to the Mill B North Fork Overlook (Hike 3).

After a short and gentle climb, you arrive at the falls at 0.15 mile. As you approach the falls, exercise caution around the slippery rocks. Return as you came.

3
MILL B NORTH FORK TRAIL TO OVERLOOK

Type of hike: Out-and-back.

See map on page 14

Total distance: 2.6 miles.
Elevation gain: 800 feet.
Maps: USGS Mount Aire.
Jurisdiction: Mount Olympus Wilderness; Wasatch National Forest.
Finding the trailhead: To reach the trailhead, drive 4.4 miles up Big Cottonwood Canyon on Utah 190. Park in the small lot located on the right (southeast) side of the road in the second, upper curve of the "S-Turn." Head up the stairs near the information signs of the parking lot, and cross the busy highway. Remember to look both ways before crossing. A trail sign is on the opposite side of the road. Additional parking and restroom facilities are at the lower parking area, which can be reached by taking the small road that branches right (southeast) from the lower curve of the "S-Turn."

Key points:
0.6 Enter the Mount Olympus Wilderness.
0.8 Take the right (east) trail through the evergreen forest.
1.3 Small trails branch right (south) to overlook area.

The hike: Several large rock outcroppings, which lie approximately one mile from the trailhead, offer hikers spectacular views of Big Cottonwood Canyon. Looking down from these rocky ledges gives you the sense of being on the top of a lofty mountain peak and may be frightening for some. Youngsters should be watched very carefully, and all hikers should keep their distances from the edge, which drops almost 600 feet to the road below.

The rocky viewing areas are visible from the trail, beyond thick oak brush, and can be reached via one of several faint paths that branch right (south) to the overlook area. Enjoy the sunshine and cool mountain air, as lounging lizards do the same. Additional wildlife seen along the route may include deer and hummingbirds.

At the trailhead sign on the north side of the highway, take the stairs to the right (east), where several switchbacks await on a warm south-facing slope. Avoid the temptation to cut switchbacks and enjoy the more gentle, established trail. The first switchback turns northwest, then the trail reaches a rock outcropping and heads into oak, maple, and juniper.

Beyond the switchbacks, the trail overlooks the Hidden Falls area and Big Cottonwood Canyon, then descends to the northeast. Follow the stream above Hidden Falls into a cool narrow canyon overgrown with willows, fir trees, and cottonwoods. Stay to the right of the creek, avoiding minor side trails crossing to the left.

Eventually, you will navigate a fairly large boulder field, watching your footing as you cross through the loose rocks, and continue on the right of the main creek. A few camping areas are visible shortly beyond the Mount Olympus Wilderness boundary sign at 0.6 mile.

The trail strays from the creek, and a fork in the trail appears at 0.8 mile. Take a right, making a wide U-turn to the south and climbing gradually through pine forest. Two switchbacks await on the sunny hillside above the shaded woodland.

As the trail levels off and turns onto a south-facing slope, watch for small trails branching to the right (south) to the overlook at 1.3 miles. The red-colored rocks of the overlook are visible through the oak and maple bordering the trail.

Head back down the same trail to the parking area.

4
DONUT FALLS TRAIL

Type of hike: Out-and-back.
Total distance: 1.6 miles.
Elevation gain: 410 feet.
Maps: USGS Mount Aire.
Jurisdiction: Wasatch National Forest.
Finding the trailhead: To reach the trailhead, drive up Big Cottonwood Canyon on Utah 190 for 9.0 miles. At this point, the road to the Donut Falls Trailhead branches to the right (south). A sign at the intersection indicates that the trailhead and its parking area is approximately one mile ahead on this road, past the Jordan Pines group picnic area and some private property. The trailhead is located at the south end of the parking lot.

Key points:
0.2 Take the small foot path branching to the creek.
0.4 Cross the bridge to west side of the creek and continue on another wide road.
0.5 Take the lower left fork.
0.7 Reach the drop-off to the creek below Donut Falls.
0.8 Reach the falls.

The hike: This short, refreshing hike skirts the Mill D South Fork Creek to Donut Falls, making it a popular destination for kids of all ages. This rugged little canyon, shaded with

Donut Falls

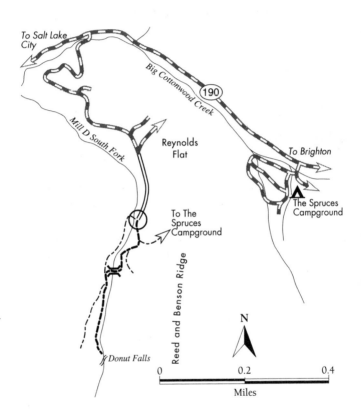

To Salt Lake City

Big Cottonwood Creek

190

Mill D South Fork

Reynolds Flat

To Brighton

The Spruces Campground

To The Spruces Campground

Reed and Benson Ridge

Donut Falls

N

0   0.2   0.4

Miles

pine and quaking aspen, is a fascinating location to visit and has much to offer families visiting the area.

At the falls, water rushes from the small creek above into what appears to be a donut hole carved in stone. The water then splashes out below, cascading over the boulders and spraying a cool mist to visiting hikers. A few minor challenges keep the trail interesting, including a short drop-off to the creek bottom below the falls. Children and elderly folks may need some help maneuvering around this obstacle.

Watch for abundant stinging nettle along the path. Avoid touching the vegetation to prevent its painful, lasting effects. Caution also should be exercised while below the falls, as many slippery rocks are found below the cascade.

From the trailhead, take the wide trail south past the wooden guard station, and continue on the main path, avoiding a side trail to the east (left), which heads to the Spruces Campground.

With some minor climbing, the trail slowly veers to the left (southeast), taking you through the shade of quaking aspen and pines. As the trail turns southwest it levels off, then heads south (left). Take the next marked footpath to the right (west) at 0.2 mile, paralleling the creek.

Avoiding small spur trails to the creek below, this path arrives at a brightly lit meadow. After crossing a minor spring, the trail wanders through the cool dark pines again.

As your journey continues, you will drop down into a little hollow. Follow the path to the right (west) and cross a nice bridge over the waterway at 0.4 mile. Pass some large boulders. Take the dirt road south (left) through a larger meadow, now following the west side of the creek.

Take the left fork (the lower road) at the trail intersection at 0.5 mile, heading south along the canyon bottom. Follow the main route heading south (avoiding a little right trail branch); the trail narrows and heads east to the creek. A rocky drop-off awaits you at 0.7 mile; beyond, you will follow the creek bottom to the falls. Carefully maneuver down the rocks to the creekbed below.

Upon reaching the falls at 0.8 mile, you may want to enjoy a snack, take a few photos, or enjoy the sunshine. Spend some quality time at this destination before returning via the same route to the trailhead.

5
SILVER LAKE
INTERPRETIVE TRAIL

Type of hike: Loop.
Total distance: 1 mile.
Elevation gain: 20 feet.
Maps: USGS Brighton.
Jurisdiction: Wasatch National Forest.
Finding the trailhead: To reach the trailhead, follow Utah 190 up Big Cottonwood Canyon for 14.7 miles from the canyon mouth. Signs indicate you are at the Silver Lake Recreation Area. Parking is available on both sides of the road. The trail begins behind the Visitor Center, on the northwest side of the building.

Key points:
0.3 Reach the northwest corner of the route and the trailhead for Lake Solitude and Twin Lakes.

The hike: Silver Lake, with its convenient access and remarkable beauty, is one of the most popular family destinations in Big Cottonwood Canyon. An amazing boardwalk trail loops through the wetlands around this sparkling alpine lake; the boardwalks protect the fragile environment, making its remarkable scenic splendor available to all. Teaming with small brook and rainbow trout, this lake is a treat for beginning anglers and children. Many families enjoy resting on

Silver Lake Interpretive Trail, Lake Solitude, and Twin Lakes

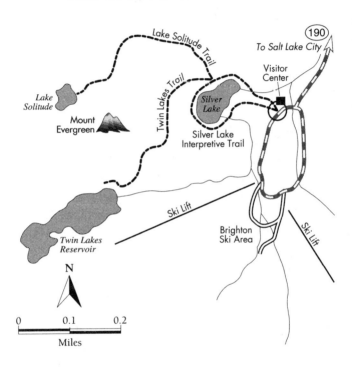

the benches and watching fish snatch bugs off the water's surface. Several fishing docks have been created to make fishing available for people with disabilities.

Meandering through marshes, quaking aspen, and pine forests, the trail provides ample views of the lake's beauty. Crossing the bridges, you may view fish swimming in the crystal clear waters. Interpretive signs provide information about the environment and the important role it plays in our lives. To maintain the beauty of this delicate ecosystem, you are asked to stay on the established trail.

Begin on the boardwalk trail, taking a right turn and heading northwest from the information signs. The path turns north and crosses a sparkling creek on a well-built bridge. Interpretive trail signs in this area discuss a fish's diet, and fish often are visible in the tributary.

The boardwalk ends along the north side of the lake, as you pass wild roses, willows, and quaking aspen. Upon reaching the northwest corner, follow the trail south along the lakeshore. Trails to Lake Solitude and Twin Lakes leave from this corner of the loop at 0.3 mile.

Resting benches and fishing docks are provided, where you can enjoy the shaded scenery. Continue south and begin a minor ascent. At the southwest corner of the lake, follow the path east in the shade of fragrant pines.

Look for abundant wildlife as the boardwalk takes you over another small stream; ducks, muskrats, and other animals may be found here. As you stroll by another fishing dock, your journey nears its end. The boardwalk returns you to the visitor center through the wetlands.

6
LAKE SOLITUDE

See map on page 24

Type of hike: Out-and-back.
Total distance: 3.4 miles (including boardwalk).
Elevation gain: 800 feet.
Maps: USGS Brighton.
Jurisdiction: Wasatch National Forest.
Finding the trailhead: To reach the trailhead, follow the Big Cottonwood Canyon road (Utah 190) for 14.7 miles from the canyon mouth. At this point, signs designate the Silver Lake Recreation Area. Parking is available on both sides of the road. The trailhead can be reached by following the Silver Lake boardwalk path for 0.3 mile, starting behind the visitor center and hiking to the northwest corner of Silver Lake (See Hike 5). A trailhead sign points the way from this location.

Key points:
0.3 Reach the northwest corner of the Silver Lake Interpretive Trail; turn right on the trail to Lake Solitude and Twin Lakes.
0.4 Take the trail heading west to Lake Solitude.
0.7 Continue on the trail heading west. Cross the Solitude single track.
1.0 Cross the jeep road; continue southwest on trail.
1.2 Follow the route as it begins to turn south (left).
1.7 Reach Lake Solitude.

The hike: Lake Solitude is an excellent destination if you seek soothing quiet in a beautiful outdoor setting. This shallow secluded lake rests quietly among pines and willows in a stunning location. Mine tailings on the opposite side of the lake remind one of the rich mining history in the canyon. Often, your only company at this lake will be a few ducks swimming to the small island. A peaceful hike to Lake Solitude includes endless groves of quaking aspen, vibrant wildflowers, and the fragrances that accompany each.

As you pass through the groves of aspen, pause to smell the bark's fragrance, listen to the rustling leaves, and feel the almost spiritual presence that accompanies them. The beauty and splendor are to be savored and remembered long after you have left. Remain on the established trails to protect the beauty for those who follow.

Sections of this route are shared with mountain bikers and caution should be exercised.

From the trailhead at the northwest corner of Silver Lake, at 0.3 mile, follow the northwest trail to the right, avoiding the left trail, which leads to Twin Lakes (Hike 7). As you stroll through the quiet stands of aspen, you may enjoy the beauty of coneflower, aster, showy daisy, columbine, and mountain ash. Sun-dotted meadows reveal elderberries, wild mushrooms, violets, and wild strawberries.

Staying on the main trail headed west (straight ahead), you will pass another trail branching left to Twin Lakes (uphill). At 0.7 mile, you will pass another downhill trail (which is Solitude's single track mountain bike trail). Next, you will cross under Solitude's Sunrise chairlift, where you may look upon the gentle green slopes of the valley below.

This path crosses a jeep road at 1.0 mile, and continues in a southwesterly direction, passing yarrow and forget-me-nots. Head south (left) at 1.2 miles, around the bend of the mountain and make a gentle descent past the "Zip A Dee Run" sign. Looking below as you approach a meadow, you will see a service road also heading up the canyon.

When you reach a fork in the trail, maintain the upper (left) trail to avoid losing altitude. The upper path undertakes a healthy climb before reaching the quiet lake at 1.7 miles. After resting, return to trailhead along the same route.

7
TWIN LAKES

See map on page 24

Type of hike: Out-and-back.
Total distance: 2.6 miles (including boardwalk).
Elevation gain: 650 feet.
Maps: USGS Brighton.
Jurisdiction: Wasatch National Forest.
Finding the trailhead: To reach the trailhead, follow Utah 190 up Big Cottonwood Canyon for 14.7 miles from the canyon mouth. Signs designate the Silver Lake Recreation Area. Parking is available on both sides of the road and the trailhead can be reached by following Silver Lake's boardwalk path for 0.3 miles from the visitor center to the northwest corner of Silver Lake (See Hike 5). A trailhead sign points the way at this location.

Key points:
- 0.3 Reach the northwest corner of Silver Lake and the trailhead for Lake Solitude and Twin Lakes.
- 0.7 Pass the remnants of an old cabin.
- 0.9 The trail turns to the right for a steep incline.
- 1.1 Upon reaching the chairlift, take the right (northwest) turn to Twin Lakes.
- 1.3 Reach Twin Lakes.

The hike: A favorite destination for many, Twin Lakes is now one large reservoir impounding water behind a massive concrete dam. This scenic area, rich in wildlife and breathtaking views, is encircled with evergreens and remarkable windswept mountain slopes. The rugged terrain surrounding the remote reservoir includes Twin Lakes Pass to the west, and Mount Evergreen to the north. Overviews of Silver Lake can be admired along the route, as well as with showy daisy, Indian paintbrush, coneflower, and wild geranium.

From the trailhead sign at the northwest corner of Silver Lake (0.3 mile), the trail heads south (left), climbing steadily up the hillside through pines. Pass the remains of an old cabin at 0.7 mile.

Elderberry, bluebell, and columbine can be appreciated as you pass a rock slide. Stay on main trail, avoiding the side trail heading right (northwest) to Lake Solitude. Showy daisy, yarrow, and lupine may greet you as the trail turns to the right (southwest).

The trail becomes moderately steep at 0.9 mile and turns northwest around a rock outcropping, then returns to the southwest. As you approach a fork in the trail at 1.1 miles, a chairlift can be seen and rushing water can be heard ahead. Take the right fork, heading northwest, and hike under the chairlift to the Twin Lakes dam access road. Follow this access road to the southeast corner of the dam and the lake at 1.3 miles.

Return as you came.

Options: Lake Solitude can be reached by continuing along the trail and taking the first right, heading north. Continuing to the west will bring you to Twin Lakes Pass, then down into Little Cottonwood Canyon and the town of Alta.

8
LAKE MARY

Type of hike: Out-and-back.
Total distance: 2.0 miles.
Elevation gain: 660 feet.
Maps: USGS Brighton.
Jurisdiction: Wasatch National Forest.
Finding the trailhead: Follow Utah 190 up Big Cottonwood Canyon for 14.4 miles to the Brighton Ski Resort and park close to the Brighton Center, near the wooden arch and information sign. The trail heads south from the east side of the big wooden sign.

Key points:
0.1 Before crossing the stream, take the left trail to the south.
0.6 The trail turns southwest.
0.8 Take the left fork to visit Dog Lake; Lake Mary lies ahead; the overlook is to the north.
1.0 Reach Lake Mary.

The hike: The trail to Lake Mary is especially popular when wildflowers are in full bloom. Flowers of all colors of the rainbow emanate from the earth, sunshine brightening their glistening petals. Along the way, you may want to visit Dog Lake, a shallow alpine lake set in a tranquil basin. Only 500 feet from the main trail, it is a nice place to stop, rest and enjoy the buzzing of insects in the meadow.

Near the Dog Lake turnoff, you can pause at another rewarding rest spot that overlooks mountain ranges and forests to the north. Large granite outcroppings, shaded by thin evergreens make this a nice stop along the way.

A cold blue lake surrounded by smooth white granite boulders, black pines and jagged mountains cutting the skyline, Lake Mary is a stunning picture. Its shimmering surface accents the blue summer skies. Many visitors return annually to experience the beauty over and over. Lake Mary is certainly a summer highlight to plan for.

This trail takes off to the south, passing under two chairlifts, and merges onto a wide road heading west (right) to some cabins. Before you cross a small stream at 0.1 mile, take the trail uphill to the left, continuing your journey south. Signs indicate that this is a section of the Great Western Trail. As you climb, shaded areas provide nice places to catch your breath.

Stay on the main trail, winding southeast above the small waterway. Bluebells, coneflowers, and wild geraniums fill the nearby meadows to the east, growing under the two chairlifts. Avoid picking these beauties to preserve them for others.

The path turns southwest at 0.6 mile and passes through granite outcroppings. Continue uphill to the southwest as the trail bends to the right, climbing around the hillside into more cool pines. You'll hear water ahead as you approach a nice granite overlook to the right (north). You also can take the short detour left (south) to Dog Lake at 0.8 mile for a well-deserved break after your climb.

Lake Mary

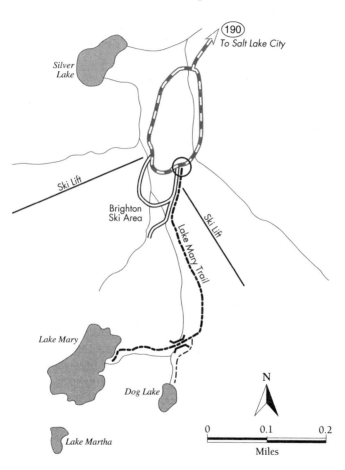

The Lake Mary trail continues ahead, crossing a wooden bridge over the small stream. Wild roses adorn the trail as you take the next left turn (the right turn takes you to Twin Lakes). The relatively flat trail follows the bend toward the sounds of water. Shortly, the Lake Mary dam can be viewed ahead, and as you approach it, the little stream can be heard to your left. Follow the path to the south side of the dam, crossing a small stream and slippery rocks to the lake's quiet shores at 1.0 mile. Return as you came.

Little Cottonwood Canyon

Little Cottonwood Canyon is a magical area, with crystal clear streams, tall dark pines, and magnificent wildflower displays. Bordered by the pristine Lone Peak Wilderness to the south and Twin Peaks Wilderness to the north, Little Cottonwood offers excellent hiking opportunities for visitors of all skill levels. The glacial activity that has carved the canyon walls has created some of the most unique hiking terrain in the area and has helped the Snowbird and Alta recreation areas become world-renowned ski resorts.

Whether you climb to Lake Catherine for spectacular wildflower displays, or rest near the still waters of Secret Lake, Little Cottonwood Canyon has much to offer. During the height of the wildflower season, Albion Basin's displays are some of the most vibrant along the Wasatch Front.

The hikes in this section of the guide vary in length and difficulty, and each is within an hour's drive of the mouth of Little Cottonwood Canyon.

Climbing through Little Cottonwood, Utah 210 takes you to all the trailheads listed herein. To reach Little Cottonwood Canyon, follow the Interstate 215 "belt loop" south (or east if you are coming from the southern and western portions of Salt Lake City) to Exit 7. Drive southeast on Utah 190. After passing Big Cottonwood Canyon, UT 190 becomes Utah 210, which takes you to the mouth of Little Cottonwood Canyon and continues to Alta. Look for road signs pointing the way to this popular recreation area.

9
TEMPLE QUARRY TRAIL

Type of hike: Loop.
Total distance: 0.3 miles.
Elevation loss: 50 feet.
Maps: USGS Draper.
Jurisdiction: Wasatch National Forest.
Finding the trailhead: Reaching the trailhead is easy. It is found at the mouth of Little Cottonwood Canyon on Utah 209, just south of UT 209's intersection with Utah 210 (the main road into the canyon). A nice parking lot with restroom facilities awaits to the east side of UT 209, between the bridge crossing Little Cottonwood Creek and the junction with UT 210. The gated parking lot (closed during the night) is in view of the lighted information sign at the canyon entrance.

Key points:
0.15 Pass the old power plant.

The hike: A wheelchair-accessible trail has recently been created at the mouth of Little Cottonwood Canyon, offering a glimpse of quarry work that was done here during the late 1800s. Granite stone was once taken from this site and used in building the Salt Lake City Temple, one of the most admired structures in the Salt Lake Valley. This pleasant trail loops through the quarry area, providing a short historical

Temple Quarry Trail

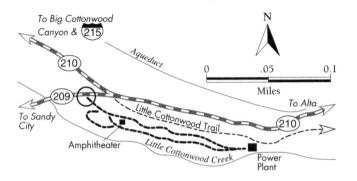

tour of the work, and allows you to gain a greater appreciation of pioneer efforts.

As you hike along the trail, which is shaded by oak and maple, you can still see markings carved in the large granite slabs left behind by the quarry workers. Although this route is short, numerous viewing possibilities await, including the chance to see mountain goats on rugged terrain to the south. An amphitheater also has been developed, where regularly scheduled presentations explain how work was conducted at this site. Interpretive signs along the route will help explain the sights to those who make this tour without the benefit of the presentations.

Begin your hike at the west end of the parking lot, beyond the restrooms. Make a gentle decent as the trail swings to the east (left). Continue left (east) past the foot path to your right (north). At the next intersection, follow the sign to the amphitheater area, which is to your left (east), and read the information provided.

As you leave the amphitheater area and approach the intersection again, take a right turn (heading southeast) toward Little Cottonwood Creek. From here, the loop is hiked in a counterclockwise direction. Numerous resting areas are available along this stretch, where you may see mountain goats on the north-facing slopes. A rock dam lies ahead.

As the trail turns north (left) at 0.15 mile, it passes an old power plant. The trail soon makes another turn to the west and returns to the parking lot where you began.

Option: For those who want a longer expedition, Little Cottonwood Trail's main trailhead is located at the east end of the quarry trail parking lot. This trail heads east into the canyon. Both hikers and bikers frequent this popular route.

10
LISA FALLS TRAIL

Type of hike: Out-and-back.
Total distance: 0.2 mile.
Elevation gain: 80 feet.
Maps: USGS Dromedary Peak.
Jurisdiction: Wasatch National Forest.
Finding the trailhead: Follow the canyon road (Utah 210) for 2.7 miles, parking on either side of the highway bend. Although the USDA Forest Service tries to maintain a trailhead sign here, vandals regularly remove or destroy it. The trail is visible heading north from the road into the shade.

Key points:
0.1 Reach Lisa Falls.

The hike: Tucked away from the highway, secluded Lisa Falls sprays a cool mist of water on hikers who venture to the north side of the rugged canyon. The falls slide over smooth granite walls; these walls also are appealing to rock climbers. This route is short, making it excellent for youngsters and less-experienced hikers who want to reach a destination quickly, yet experience the challenges of an unpaved path and a little climbing.

Hidden among maples and pines, the surprise of the falls is a worthwhile goal. The gentle waters cool this area in the summertime, making it a nice spot for children and their

Lisa Falls Trail, Little Cottonwood Trail

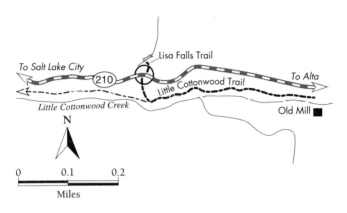

parents. It also is a popular place to stop before continuing up the canyon for a picnic, another hike, or a scenic drive.

Heading north from the highway, this shady path climbs through maples, oak and pine trees. This route is fairly straightforward, with little chance of getting lost. The rocks in the path can be exciting for youngsters as they maneuver around them to reach the destination. Shortly, you will arrive at a dry creekbed. Watch for slippery areas as you near the falls at 0.1 mile.

Return to the trailhead, following the same route.

11
LITTLE COTTONWOOD TRAIL

Type of hike: Out-and-back.
Total distance: 1.6 miles.
Elevation loss: 170 feet.
Maps: USGS Dromedary Peak.
Jurisdiction: Wasatch National Forest.

See map on page 40

Finding the trailhead: To locate the trailhead, follow the canyon road (Utah 210) for 2.7 miles to the trailhead parking area. Parking is found on both sides of the highway bend. Although the USDA Forest Service tries to maintain a trailhead sign near the trail, vandals remove or destroy it regularly. The trail is visible heading south of the road; it continues downhill toward Little Cottonwood Creek.

Key points:
0.1 Take the left (east) turn at the junction below the trailhead.
0.6 Pass metal posts and large boulders.
0.8 Reach the old mill.

The hike: The remains of an old mill lie near the cool waters of Little Cottonwood Creek, a quiet reminder of years past, when the creek's power was harnessed to do the work of many. Today, the ghostly foundations, smothered by vegetation, whisper the tales of early canyon inhabitants.

Although this route does not begin at the Little Cottonwood trailhead at the canyon mouth, some of the most rewarding and pleasant sections of the trail are along this relatively short stretch. The width of the path makes it easy for families to use while enjoying each other's company, although caution should be exercised to allow faster-moving mountain bikes to pass.

Begin just past the granite stones near the parking area, where the wide trail gently drops into pines and maples. At the junction at 0.1 mile, take the left (uphill) path heading east through the cottonwoods. Looking to the south you can see steep jagged slopes of the granite mountains.

Continue along the path, which is shaded by pines, chokecherry, river birch, and willow. Looking south into an open side canyon, you can spot a good-sized waterfall in the distance.

Pass a couple of metal posts at 0.6 mile as you follow the north bank of Little Cottonwood Creek. A rocky area stands to your left along with some mountain mahogany. Walking around large boulders, you can see crystal-clear water dancing over the rocks and cold dark pools in the adjacent creek.

Soon, you arrive at a spot across the creek from the old mill (0.8 mile). Here you may rest, take a few photographs of the old foundations, and wonder about the work that occurred here many years ago. Avoid attempting to cross the slippery rocks and dangerously cold water to get a closer look at the building. Its ghostly stillness is best viewed from this point.

Return to the trailhead as you came.

12
BARRIER FREE TRAIL

Type of hike: Out-and-back.
Total distance: 0.8 mile.
Elevation gain: 70 feet.
Maps: USGS Dromedary Peak.
Jurisdiction: Snowbird Ski and Summer Resort.
Finding the trailhead: To reach the trailhead, drive 6.5 miles up Little Cottonwood Canyon on Utah 210 to Entry 2 of Snowbird Ski and Summer Resort. The trail begins from the third level of the Snowbird Center. After you follow the wheelchair ramp, head south toward the ski mountain. You will follow a few gentle switchbacks and cross a mountain bike trail before reaching the official trailhead. Avoid the temptation to cut the switchbacks, and preserve the beauty for others to enjoy.

Key points:
0.4 Reach the overlook deck.

The hike: Stroller and accessible to persons with disabilities, the interpretive signs along Snowbird's Barrier Free nature trail will remind you of how nature interacts with man. As you walk the path, you will see a myriad of flowers filling the meadows, including coneflower, wild geranium, Indian paintbrush, and showy daisy. A wooden deck, offering cool breezes and glimpses of the valley below, is at trail's end.

Barrier Free Trail

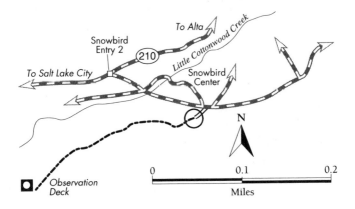

Although the route can be covered in a matter of minutes, it is worthwhile to take your time, enjoy the charm of the area, and chat with family members about what you are seeing and learning. The route passes through several different habitats and signs teach visitors about a number of unique topics, including the water cycle, what animals eat, and how habitat interacts with wildlife.

From the trailhead, follow the paved path as it wanders west to the deck area. Your first interpretive sign discusses the changing meadows. Remember to enjoy the beauty of this environment without leaving reminders of your visit for others. Take advantage of the numerous resting points to visit with your children about what you see. After reaching the overlook at 0.4 mile, return to the trailhead.

13
ALBION MEADOWS TRAIL

Type of hike: Out-and-back.
Total distance: 2 miles.
Elevation gain: 650 feet.
Maps: USGS Brighton.
Jurisdiction: Wasatch National Forest; Alta Ski Area.
Finding the trailhead: Travel approximately 8.3 miles up Little Cottonwood Canyon on Utah 210 to the town of Alta. Trail-head parking is available along UT 210 or in a large lot near the Albion Day Lodge and Ski Shop. Be sure to park legally to avoid problems when you return. You can pick up the trail south of the Snow Pine Lodge Restaurant and restrooms; it heads southeast. You also may note the two chairlifts nearby.

Key points:
0.1 The trail turns south, climbing uphill.
0.3 Take a narrow foot path to east (left) into the willows.
0.5 Cross the gate blocking vehicle traffic and go west to return to the main service road.
0.6 Continue uphill (to the south) on the service road.
1.0 Reach the fork in the road; one way leads to the restaurant, the other to the Albion Basin Campground. Return to the trailhead from this point.

Albion Meadows Trail, Secret Lake Trail, and Sugarloaf Road

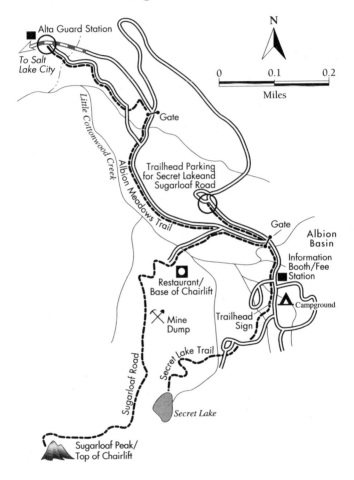

N

0   0.1   0.2

Miles

Alta Guard Station

To Salt Lake City

Little Cottonwood Creek

Albion Meadows Trail

Gate

Trailhead Parking for Secret Lake and Sugarloaf Road

Gate

Albion Basin

Information Booth/Fee Station

Restaurant/ Base of Chairlift

Campground

Mine Dump

Trailhead Sign

Sugarloaf Road

Secret Lake Trail

Secret Lake

Sugarloaf Peak/ Top of Chairlift

The hike: The Albion Meadows Trail, near Alta Ski Area, is one of the most spectacular hikes your family can take during the hiking season. Vibrant colors fill the gentle meadows in summer, making for one of the most memorable easy hikes in the area.

Although several other trails reach from Alta to spectacular vistas and quiet, hidden lakes, this gentle trail should provide you and your family with some of the finest colors of the area, with only a fraction of the sweat and effort found on the others.

This is one of those hikes where the destination is the trail itself. Anytime is a great time to turn back, if you have had your fill of blooms and sunshine. Trail improvements are ongoing and may change sections of this spectacular journey, but the general direction is expected to remain the same. To capture the essence of the day, bring a camera and plenty of film.

After beginning your journey from the trailhead to the southeast, the road that serves as the trail quickly turns right (south), leading through a green meadow at 0.1 mile. Upon reaching the top of a small hill, the trail becomes level. Shortly, you cross a small stream and pass twice under one of the chairlifts.

As you cross under the chairlift again, be on the lookout for a small but well-defined path branching to the left at 0.3 mile. Here, you have an option to take a less steep but longer trail. Otherwise, continue on the main road upward.

This small foot path follows a wide turn around evergreen trees and for a short distance, runs parallel to the main road to Albion Basin, before entering pines and small willows. It eventually returns to the west and meets with the service road that you previously left. As you pass a locked gate that blocks the road to vehicle traffic at 0.5 mile, you should hear a babbling brook ahead.

This level section is highlighted by the sound of cascading water. Cross under the two chairlifts again, and follow the main route uphill (south), ignoring side trails.

Passing tall cool pines, you will view a granite rock outcropping to the left and golden-colored mine tailings on the east hill. Views of rugged mountains are abundant and Little Cottonwood Creek can be heard through the willows to the west.

If you are quiet, you might view spectacular wildlife among the lush vegetation. Hummingbirds frequent the area, drinking the sweet nectar, and deer can be seen resting around the dark pines. This section is one of the most spectacular of your journey.

When you reach a fork in the road at 1 mile, you must decide where to go. This is a great place to return to your vehicle. Scanning the area from this location, you may spot several mine dumps, the chairlift to the east, and an abundance of nature's fireworks.

Options: Several other destinations lie nearby. If you go to the right (west), you may walk to Alf's Restaurant, which is closed during the summer. The left (east) road takes you to Albion Basin Campground, and eventually to Secret Lake.

14
SECRET LAKE TRAIL

See map on page 46

Type of hike: Out-and-back.
Total distance: 2.4 miles round trip.
Elevation gain: 450 feet.
Maps: USGS Brighton.
Jurisdiction: Wasatch National Forest.
Finding the trailhead: Drive 10.8 miles up Little Cottonwood Canyon on Utah 210. The last two miles, beyond the town of Alta, are traveled on a gravel road suitable for two-wheel-drive vehicles. Parking is available near the top of the Sunnyside chairlift. A large information sign at that location will help you orient yourself.

Key points:
0.3 Continue along gravel road, avoiding branches to left and right.
0.5 Arrive at the campground fee station; look for the trail-head sign to the right shortly beyond.
1.0 Pass a small mine dump. Take the right switchback to the north. The path ahead is a dead end.
1.2 Arrive at the lake.

The hike: Children will enjoy hiking to Secret Lake. The distance is short, yet challenging enough to give them a sense of accomplishment once they reach this sparkling hidden treasure. Tucked away from view until the end of the trail, this adventure rewards all visitors with a pristine setting for meditation, relaxation, and peace. Interpretive signs along the route add to the experience, providing information on wildflower identification and the importance of our precious resources.

Located at the base of Sugarloaf Peak, large boulders surround the shallow lake which, later in the season, can see a significant drop in its water level. Low-growth shrubs and willows surround sections of the lake, set below the jagged cliffs. Early in the season, mosquitos can be merciless. Bring plenty of insect repellant to ensure a longer stay without excessive bites and distractions.

Starting at the Sunnyside chairlift parking area, begin walking along the gravel road to the south (this is sometimes closed to vehicles). An abundance of wildflowers are visible along the route, their blues, reds, pinks, and whites set against the rich green foliage. Indian paintbrush, coneflower, and forget-me-nots adorn this section of trail.

As you walk along the road, you will pass branching roads to the left and right at 0.3 mile. Below to the right (west), lies a closed restaurant and the base of the Sugarloaf chairlift, where the Sugarloaf Road continues (Hike 15). The road to the left goes to an old mine dump and trailhead for Lake Catherine.

As you continue south on the main road, you will reach the fee station for the Albion Basin Campground at 0.5 mile. A trailhead sign can be seen to the right, just beyond the station, indicating the distance to the lake is 1.0 mile.

As you work your way west, you will cross a little bridge, and later, a service road. The trail begins to climb through bluebells, fireweed, and Indian paintbrush and soon you pass the first interpretive sign.

This beautiful trail continues west, crossing under the Supreme chairlift and passing beautiful fragile columbine. Numerous confusing spur trails cross the main path, but you should continue west, following the signs pointing to the actual route. The Secret Lake Trail, six to eight feet wide, eventually takes you to the second interpretive sign that discusses water.

You will reach a more open area where small waterfalls may be visible early in the season. As the trail climbs, you pass a little mine dump. Take the right fork at 1.0 mile, located near a large sheet of rock. The left fork ahead goes to a dead end. A few more steep switchbacks will take you to the quiet lake destination at 1.2 miles.

Return as you came.

15
SUGARLOAF ROAD

Type of hike: Out-and-back.

See map on page 46

Total distance: 5.2 miles.
Elevation gain: 1,110 feet.
Maps: USGS Brighton; USGS Dromedary Peak.
Jurisdiction: Wasatch National Forest; Alta Ski Area.
Finding the trailhead: Arrive at the trailhead parking area by driving 10.8 miles up Little Cottonwood Canyon on Utah 210. The last two miles, beyond the town of Alta, are traveled on a gravel road, suitable for two-wheel-drive vehicles. Parking is available near the top of the Sunnyside chairlift. A large information sign at that location will help you orient yourself.

Key points:
0.2 Take the road branching to right (west), heading to the restaurant and the bottom of the Sugarloaf chairlift.
0.6 The trail begins a steady climb, following several switchbacks.
1.3 Reach the end of the switchbacks; trail climbs to the south.
1.8 Pass a significant mine dump with remnants of wooden structures.
2.0 Cross through the mountain pass to the west.
2.2 Take the main road (left fork), heading southwest.

2.3 Take left (south) fork again, eventually turning east to the top of the Sugarloaf chairlift.
2.6 Reach the end of the trail near the top of the Sugarloaf chairlift.

The hike: Hiking the Sugarloaf Road, a service road that gently climbs through open wet meadows, rocky hillsides, and past several abandoned mines, leads to one of the easiest views overlooking American Fork Canyon.

The trail, which passes near many remnants of the area's rich mining history, gradually climbs to the divide overlooking American Fork Canyon, Mount Timpanogos, and Hidden Peak. Fortunately, the mine shafts have been gated for everyone's safety. In addition to the mine remains, alpine wildflowers dot the hillsides, and it is interesting to see how the vegetation and wildlife changes as you climb to the end of this trail, which is near the top of the Sugarloaf chairlift.

This trail is shared with mountain bikers and caution should be exercised while climbing this route. Earlier in the season, snow covers sections of trail and you should be careful as you cross slippery areas. You should also pace yourself to adjust to the high elevation. Bring plenty of drinking water, mosquito repellant, and sun block, as well.

Starting at the Sunnyside chairlift parking area, begin by walking along the gravel road to the south, which is sometimes closed to vehicles. Indian paintbrush, coneflower, and forget-me-nots adorn this section of trail. As you walk along the road, you will encounter other roads that branch to the left and right. Below you to the right (west) lies Alf's Restaurant and the base of the Sugarloaf chairlift. Turn right (west) at 0.2 mile on this trail, passing through the beautiful meadow, and head to the chairlift.

At 0.6 mile, near the base of the mountain and behind the restaurant and chairlift, take a wide service road that begins a steady ascent to the northwest. Several switchbacks later, at 1.3 miles, the trail heads south. You will pass a mine dump and remnants of this area's mining history at 1.8 miles. Later, the road climbs under the chairlift. Continuing steadily uphill, at 2.0 miles the trail makes a turn to the west through a pass.

Beyond the pass, you reach a fork in the road at 2.2 miles. Take the main left road to the southwest. At the next fork at 2.3 miles, take another left, heading to the south. As the trail approaches the ridge at 2.6 miles, it turns east to the top of the Sugarloaf chairlift. From here, you can enjoy the surrounding views before returning to the trailhead.

16
LAKE CATHERINE

Type of hike: Out-and-back.
Total distance: 2.6 miles.
Elevation gain: 740 feet.
Maps: USGS Brighton.
Jurisdiction: Wasatch National Forest.
Finding the trailhead: To reach the trailhead, drive 10.8 miles up Little Cottonwood Canyon on Utah 210. The last two miles, beyond the town of Alta, are traveled on a gravel road suitable for two-wheel-drive vehicles. Parking is available near the top of the Sunnyside chairlift. A large information sign at that location will help you orient yourself. If the gate is open, you can drive to a closer trailhead parking area, which is 0.2 miles farther along the road and to the left (east). From this second trailhead parking area, head east toward the mountainside to begin your hike.

Key points:
0.5 Before the trail heads east, stop at a great overlook point to admire view.
0.7 Enter a big wet meadow.
1.0 Cross Catherine Pass.
1.3 Reach Lake Catherine.

The hike: Hikers of all ages seem to enjoy the trail from Albion Basin to Lake Catherine. Meadows of wildflowers, a shim-

Lake Catherine

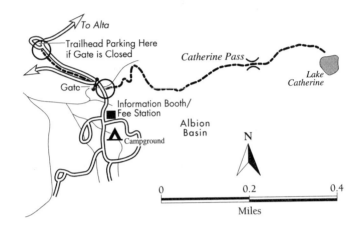

mering alpine lake, and abundant wildlife are all aspects to be absorbed. During my last visit, students from several universities had gathered here to study the geological wonders of this area.

As with other hikes in this area, this route offers superb displays of wildflowers. In addition, wildlife is abundant and mining remnants can be spotted. A camera is a must, as are mosquito repellant, sunblock, and water.

This description begins at the second trailhead, which is 0.2 mile southeast of the Sunnyside chairlift parking area. Start by walking east through the meadow. You will begin to hear the refreshing sound of water cascading in background as you take in the tapestry of purple, red, yellow, and white set on green.

From the dirt road, you will see the trail sign pointing the way to your ascent. On the first switchback, approximately 50 feet off the trail, you will see a wooden building and rock wall sealing off a mine shaft.

The colors continue as you climb steadily past several switchbacks through willows and humid conditions. Admire the valley view as you approach a nice shaded overlook at 0.5 mile. Beyond the viewpoint the trail heads east, following a small stream. Columbines and asters cover the area as you pass below a mine dump and rocky outcropping. Your route continues on a switchback to northeast, climbing through alpine meadows, fir trees, and more rock outcroppings. Finches and hummingbirds may be spotted here. Cross a small stream.

A large wet meadow covered in elephantheads and bluebells opens up at 0.7 mile. Upon crossing another small stream and passing a big rock at the end of this wet meadow, you begin climbing a fairly steep section to Catherine Pass.

When you reach the top of the steep section at 1.0 mile, the trail turns right (south) to the top of the pass. Here, you cross the Great Western Trail and can look down on Lake Catherine.

To get to the lake, drop down to the north. The route turns east (right) as you approach several rocky outcroppings. Before the bog, a rocky area indicates where you can hike south to the lake, which is reached at 1.3 miles.

Enjoy the lake before returning as you came.

American Fork Canyon

American Fork Canyon is a treasure house of beautiful hikes reaching from the Lone Peak Wilderness Area on the north to Mount Timpanogos Wilderness Area on the south. Whether the destination is Silver Lake's quiet shoreline, or underground stalactites found in Timpanogos Cave, canyon visitors will agree that this rugged mountainous region has much to offer.

The popular Alpine Loop (Utah 92) climbs through this magnificent landscape, wandering through the pine and aspen forests while providing spectacular views and hiking opportunities for visitors of all ages.

This canyon has become a very popular recreational area and has received extensive use over the past decade. To maintain the beauty of this canyon, a minor day-use fee is charged at the canyon mouth to fund repairs and improvements.

Many of the hikes in this section have been chosen for their relatively short trail lengths, relatively less steep inclines, and unique views. Although all of the hikes vary in length and difficulty, each is within an hour's drive of Interstate 15 at Exit 287.

To reach American Fork Canyon, travel south from Salt Lake City on I-15 into northern Utah County. From Exit 287, drive 7.4 miles east on UT 92 to the mouth of American Fork Canyon, where you are greeted by the information/fee station. From this point, follow the directions provided in the Finding the Trailhead section of each hike to reach your desired destination.

17
BATTLE CREEK FALLS

Type of hike: Out-and-back.
Total distance: 1.8 miles.
Elevation gain: 460 feet.
Maps: USGS Orem.
Jurisdiction: Uinta National Forest.
Cautions: Be aware that this trail is shared with horses and mountain bikers.
Finding the trailhead: Drive 7.4 miles east on Utah 92 from Interstate 15/Exit 287 to the mouth of American Fork Canyon. Just as UT 92 enters the canyon, Utah 146 branches uphill to the right (south). Take UT 146 (which becomes 100 East in Pleasant Grove) 4.8 miles south to Pleasant Grove's 200 South, passing the Pleasant Grove Ranger District office at 4.4 miles. From 200 South and Second East (Battle Creek Road), turn left (east) on Battle Creek Road and drive 2.0 miles, passing the large water tank, to the trailhead at Kiwanis Park, located at the east end of Battle Creek Road. You may want to view the monument in the park, which memorializes the skirmish between Native Americans and settlers that took place here.

Key points:
0.5 Cross the bridge.
0.6 Pass the small cave.
0.9 Reach the area above the waterfall and breather pipe.

Battle Creek Falls

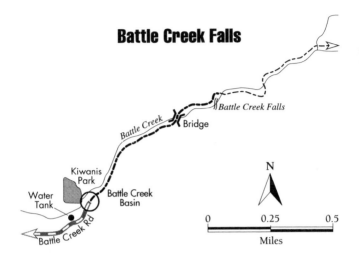

The hike: Battle Creek Canyon offers a unique experience for all visitors, providing a wide diversity of terrains, vistas, and elevation changes. Hikers of all skill levels can enjoy the beauty found in this ecosystem, and can look forward to numerous wildlife viewing opportunities along the way.

This route climbs along a beautiful cascading stream to Battle Creek Falls, where the water drops hundreds of feet and sprays a cool mist to nearby travelers. A breather pipe above the falls splashes bursts of water for children to play in. Near the cool creek, wild roses and other wildflowers color the landscape. Just above the falls, numerous trees provide shade for a quiet rest before the return hike.

Battle Creek attracts numerous trail users, requiring courtesy from all. Other travelers include equestrians and mountain bikers. Although the breather pipe may be entertaining, caution should be exercised so that unexpected noises don't spook nearby horses, potentially causing injury. You also may find poison ivy or oak along the trail. Loose rocks in the trail may slow travel, but caution may prevent a twisted ankle or a fall. Bring plenty of drinking water.

Begin your hike at the south end of Kiwanis Park, on a jeep road that leads into the canyon mouth. Heading northeast into the canyon, you may see dragonflies darting around the trees, seeking a mosquito meal. Rugged rock ledges tower above as you follow the jeep road into the canyon.

Continuing up the trail, you will begin to hear water ahead. As you proceed, the jeep trail narrows and the noisy creek makes itself visible. The trail eventually will take you to a wooden bridge, which crosses to the left side of the creek at 0.5 mile. Beyond, the trail becomes steeper.

On the left side of the trail at 0.6 mile, you will find a hole in the rock wall. Children may want to take a look inside, providing a perfect rest stop for tired parents.

Shortly beyond, you will catch your first glimpse of the magnificent waterfall rushing over a rock ledge. Climb the next steep section to get above this waterfall at 0.9 mile for a panoramic view of the valley below. After admiring the splendor of this area, return to trailhead via the same route.

Options: Continuing up the canyon takes you along an old pipeline, where you can see more breather pipes, smaller waterfalls, tall dark pine trees, and lush wildflowers along the cascading creek. You may find this less-traveled section to be more enjoyable than the first section, although many parts are steep and loose rocks cover parts of the trail.

18
FIVE SENSES NATURE TRAIL

Type of hike: Out-and-back.
Total distance: 0.4 mile.
Elevation gain: 40 feet.
Maps: USGS Timpanogos Cave.
Jurisdiction: Timpanogos Cave National Monument.
Finding the trailhead: Drive 7.4 miles east on Utah 92 from Interstate 15/Exit 287 to the information/fee station at the mouth of American Fork Canyon. Approximately 2.1 miles after entering the canyon mouth, look for a bridge on the left (north) side of the road, just past highway mile marker 10 and the pedestrian crossing sign. The Timpanogos Cave National Monument visitor center parking area is to the right (south). A sign on the bridge crossing the American Fork River points to the path to Swinging Bridge Picnic Area. Parking is available at the trailhead, near the visitor center, and along the river beyond the visitor center. Access for persons with disabilities is located at the parking lot before the visitor center, approximately 0.2 mile before the bridge. Disabled visitors should be aware that some parts of the trail may be moderately challenging.

Key points:
0.2 Arrive at the picnic area.

Five Senses Nature Trail, Timpanogos Cave Trail

The hike: A pleasant surprise lies across the street from the Timpanogos Cave National Monument Visitor Center. The Five Senses Nature Trail is a short, easy trail that is accessible to people with disabilities and provides a wonderful recreational learning activity for the entire family. Although the trail can be traveled in minutes, great opportunities await those who slow down, spend a little time, and enjoy the beauty that American Fork Canyon has to offer.

Numbered signs along the trail identify stopping points, which are described in free brochures that are available at the visitor center. These points are excellent places to view, listen, touch, and smell nature, as well as better understand and reflect upon the impact man has on his environment.

After crossing the bridge with the sign pointing to Swinging Bridge Picnic Area, follow the paved path that switchbacks up the hill. Stone stair steps are available if you want to take a short cut on this already very short trail.

Look for the unique characteristics of the trees, rocks, and plants as your path winds to the west. The trail winds through different areas of the forest, including a riparian area near the river, heavily forested areas, and open meadows. You also will have opportunities to view rock slides, damage from floods, and impacts of man on the environment. Vegetation along the path includes maple, cottonwood, snowberry, wild rose, elderberry, penstemon, Oregon grape, goldenrod, juniper, oak, sagebrush, dogwood, thistle, stinging nettle, mullein, and ragweed.

Upon reaching the picnic area at 0.2 mile, enjoy the shade and a snack before returning. Restrooms are available at that location. Return to trailhead following the same route.

19
TIMPANOGOS CAVE TRAIL

See map on page 63

Type of hike: Out-and-back.
Total distance: 3.0 miles.
Elevation gain: 1,070 feet.
Maps: USGS Timpanogos Cave.
Jurisdiction: Timpanogos Cave National Monument.
Cautions: Watch for falling rocks and if you plan to tour the cave, give yourself plenty of time to reach the cave entrance.
Finding the trailhead: Drive 7.4 miles east on Utah 92 from Interstate 15/Exit 287 to the information/fee station at the mouth of American Fork Canyon. Continue east for approximately 2.1 miles after entering the canyon mouth, to the Timpanogos Cave National Monument Visitor Center on the right (south). Parking is available near the visitor center and along the river beyond the visitor center.

Key points:
0.4 Pass through the tunnel.
0.8 Reach the halfway marker.
1.1 Reach the three-quarter way marker.
1.5 Arrive at the cave entrance.

The hike: One of the most popular hikes in American Fork Canyon leads to the "heart" of Mount Timpanogos, which is found in Timpanogos Cave. Open to visitors during the summer months, this relatively strenuous hike takes you to the cave's entrance, where guided tours are available. Due to the cave's popularity, you are advised to make reservations for tours in advance. Call (801) 756-5238 to make a reservation.

This treasure house is full of beautiful stalactites, underground pools, and other formations that amaze and mystify. For thousands of years, delicate and beautiful mineral formations have been developing, one drop at a time, in these hidden chambers of darkness.

Although Timpanogos Cave provides spectacular viewing opportunities of nature at work, exploring these caverns is only part of the experience. Located 1.5 miles beyond the trailhead, most visitors hike this distance to explore one of Mother Nature's wonders, but others hike this trail daily for exercise and magnificent views. Wonderful sightseeing opportunities are available as you climb to the grotto. Rising above the floor of American Fork Canyon, this smooth, paved path wanders past beautiful wildflowers and overlooks the canyon below.

The trail winds along the north-facing slope of the canyon, and numerous resting points are available. You are encouraged to bring plenty of water for the hike and a jacket for the cool (43 degrees) temperatures inside the cave. Cavern tours travel through three different chambers and generally last an hour (in addition to the hiking time). As a National Park Service Area, everything is protected, including all rocks, minerals, and vegetation growing along the trail. Baby strollers and other wheeled vehicles are not allowed on the trail system.

Follow the paved path past the safety warnings and informational signs. Caution should be exercised in marked areas where the potential for falling rock is high. Upon passing the first rock slide area, shade awaits for a cool rest.

As you approach a bend overlooking the canyon, the trail becomes steeper. A nearby sign discusses how the canyon was carved by the river below. At the next switchback, another overlook area offers a picturesque resting point. Pass the quarter-way marker at 0.4 mile as you hike through a short tunnel blasted through the rock.

After passing a crystal-like rock outcropping at signpost 14, the trail continues to reach the halfway point at 0.8 mile. Squirrels scamper across the trail and visitors are often greeted by a pleasant canyon breeze.

Numerous rock slide areas are passed as you continue climbing. The cave entrance may also be viewed ahead. Passing the three-quarter marker at 1.1 miles, the trail is still very steep. A stone restroom stands just off the trail ahead. After a few more turns, the cave entrance greets you at 1.5 miles. Tours begin here. After taking the tour or an enjoyable rest, return to visitor center along the same route.

20
TIBBLE FORK LOOP TRAIL

Type of hike: Loop.
Total distance: 3.8 miles.
Elevation gain: 911 feet.
Maps: USGS Timpanogos Cave and USGS Aspen Grove.
Jurisdiction: Uinta National Forest.
Cautions: Be aware that this trail is shared with mountain bikers and horseback riders.
Finding the trailhead: Drive 7.4 miles east on Utah 92 from Interstate 15/Exit 287 to the information/fee station at the mouth of American Fork Canyon. Continue east into American Fork Canyon for approximately 4.6 miles to where the North Fork/Utah 144 branches to the left (north). Drive 2.2 miles up the North Fork to the dam of Tibble Fork Reservoir. Parking is available near the dam.

Key points:
1.0 Cross the log jam.
1.3 Cross a second dry creek.
1.7 Reach the second large meadow.
2.0 Meet the connecting trail to Mill Canyon.
2.2 Pass an abandoned beaver pond.
2.8 Meet the Mill Canyon Trail, continue downhill.
3.4 Cross the stream.
3.6 Cross the inlet to Tibble Fork.
3.8 Return to the trailhead.

Tibble Fork Loop Trail

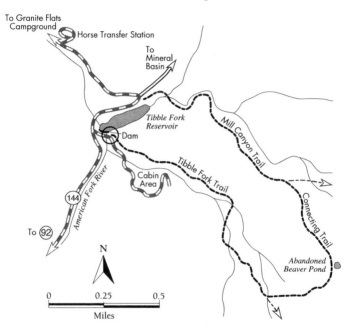

The hike: Families looking for a nice evening hike should consider the Tibble Fork Loop Trail, which begins near Tibble Fork Dam and returns near the inlet of the little blue-green reservoir.

You will note changes in plant communities, temperatures, and abundance of water as the trail takes you from the drier, warmer southwest side of the mountain to the cooler, wetter northeast side. Color should be abundant throughout the year, with a rainbow of wildflowers in the spring and summer. As the air becomes crisp in the autumn, you may see large numbers of golden aspens and crimson maples, outlined with dark green pines.

The trail can be reached by walking east across the dam. At pavement's end, you will notice a large conglomerate rock and a trail climbing to the southeast on a fairly steep incline, rising above the road to the summer cabin area.

The trail begins on the west side of a mountain and climbs though several switchbacks in oak, sagebrush and maple. (Avoid cutting the switchbacks to minimize erosion.) You then climb steadily southeast, onto the south side of the mountain, and enter groves of maples.

At 1.0 mile, you cross a fairly large log jam in a nearly dry creekbed. In the spring or during severe thunderstorms, the creek fills with water, creating a hazard for backcountry travelers. Climb the next hillside, heading southwest, to another dry streambed at 1.3 miles, where the trail rises quickly through quaking aspen. This is one of the steepest sections of the route.

Eventually the trail levels out and you arrive at a large, fairly wet meadow. A gentle climb takes you to a larger meadow to the southeast at 1.7 miles. Plenty of mosquitoes await, but spectacular views compensate for their presence.

You arrive at a trail sign pointing to Mill Canyon Trail at 2.0 miles, shortly beyond the second meadow, as the trail heads southeast and rises a little. Take this connecting trail to the left (north), following it up another gentle ascent to an abandoned beaver pond at 2.4 miles.

This trail then begins a fast descent through quaking

aspen and pines to Mill Canyon Trail at 2.8 miles. Continue downhill/northwest on the Mill Creek Trail to Tibble Fork Reservoir. Sections of this path are very wet and muddy, and the stream babbles to the right as you proceed.

At 3.4 miles, the stream crosses your path and you must ford it. A small trail heading left avoids this crossing for a few minutes, but will not prevent you from getting your feet wet. A large red-colored rock towers above and willows line the stream. After cooling your feet two more times in the stream, you arrive at the American Fork River as it feeds into Tibble Fork Reservoir at 3.6 miles.

Returning to your vehicle requires crossing the American Fork River and walking along the north side of the lake to the trailhead, or returning along the south side of the lake to the trail's beginning at 3.8 miles.

Options: Tibble Fork Reservoir offers other opportunities for outdoor fun. You may enjoy watching the fish rising in the lake, a young angler trying to catch a wary trout, or the serene views of the canyon.

21
SILVER LAKE

Type of hike: Out-and-back.
Total distance: 3.8 miles.
Elevation gain: 1,300 feet.
Maps: USGS Dromedary Peak.
Jurisdiction: Lone Peak Wilderness Area; Uinta National Forest.
Finding the trailhead: Drive 7.4 miles east on Utah 92 from Interstate 15/Exit 287 to the information/fee station at the mouth of American Fork Canyon. Continue east into American Fork Canyon for approximately 4.6 miles past the fee station to where the North Fork/Utah 144 branches to the left (north). Drive 2.2 miles up the North Fork to Tibble Fork Reservoir. The road continues past the northeast end of the reservoir, then switchbacks to the west, toward the Granite Flats Campground area. At a point beyond the horse transfer station but before the campground, take the dirt road to the right, following the signs that direct you to Silver Lake Flat Reservoir. The road climbs numerous switchbacks on a dry hillside, then enters groves of aspen and passes a summer cabin area. At 3.8 miles from the Granite Flats turnoff, you will arrive at Silver Lake Flat Reservoir. Abundant parking is available at the trailhead north of the reservoir. The trail is visible heading into a grove of quaking aspen; it begins to the right (east) of the restrooms and is the main (left) trail heading north.

Silver Lake

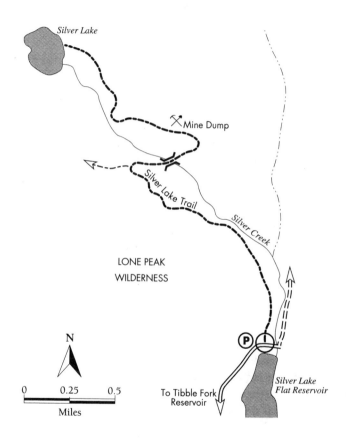

Silver Lake

Mine Dump

Silver Lake Trail

Silver Creek

LONE PEAK
WILDERNESS

N

0   0.25   0.5
Miles

P I

To Tibble Fork
Reservoir

*Silver Lake
Flat Reservoir*

Key points:

0.4 Cross a small stream.
0.5 Enter the Lone Peak Wilderness.
0.9 The trail turns east.
1.3 The trail heads north.
1.5 Pass near a mine dump.
1.9 Arrive at Silver Lake.

The hike: Access to Silver Lake recently has become much easier, thanks to hard working volunteers and employees of the USDA Forest Service. This trail, now an enjoyable journey though stands of quaking aspen and wildflower meadows, takes you to a spectacular alpine lake, enclosed by jagged, rocky cliffs.

The newly constructed section of trail furnishes remarkable vistas of Silver Lake Flat and surrounding mountains, and allows hikers of all abilities to reach this remote lake in the heart of the Lone Peak Wilderness Area.

This route is well-marked and takes you through tall, quiet groves of quaking aspen that are dotted with large granite boulders and numerous wildflowers. Babbling Silver Creek calms the ears as you climb. Open meadows are alive with colors and fragrances throughout the summer. As autumn approaches, aspen leaves turn to gold, making for a spectacular fall adventure.

Arriving at trail's end, you will note very short subalpine fir trees and steep rocky slopes enclosing a crystal clear blue-green alpine lake. A waterfall feeds the lake part of the year and snowbanks can be numerous along the north shore. You also may notice very small brook trout rising to flies on the surface, breaking the water's stillness.

Begin your journey on the well-marked trail amid the aspen and boulders. A small stream can be heard to your right (east). Pass brightly lit meadows full of colorful vegetation as you continue.

After crossing a log bridge over a small creek at 0.4 miles, arrive at the Lone Peak Wilderness Area boundary and the trail register (0.5 mile). Campfires are not permitted and group size is limited to 15 people to protect this fragile environment.

Beyond the wilderness sign, your path heads northeast, leading through glowing multi-colored meadows and more quiet groves of quaking aspen. At 0.9 mile, the trail turns east. This improved section of trail rises gradually, crosses a wooden bridge over the creek, and offers spectacular vistas of the valley below.

At 1.3 miles, the trail switches back to the north and resumes a course to the lake, following the warmer and drier east side of the valley. Cross a mine dump at 1.5 miles, the pass some small beaver ponds, and a modest waterfall.

Just before you arrive at the blue-green lake at 1.9 miles, a few short switchbacks take you up the steepest part of the journey, with stone steps to facilitate your climb.

After enjoying the spectacular setting, return to trailhead by following the same route.

22
FOREST LAKE

Type of hike: Out-and-back.
Total distance: 3.8 miles.
Elevation gain: 1,000 feet.
Maps: USGS Brighton.
Jurisdiction: Uinta National Forest.
Finding the trailhead: Drive 7.4 miles east on Utah 92 from Interstate 15/Exit 287 to the information/fee station at the mouth of American Fork Canyon. Continue east into American Fork Canyon for approximately 4.6 miles past the fee station to where the North Fork/Utah 144 branches to the left (north). Drive 2.2 miles up the North Fork to Tibble Fork Reservoir. Follow the road along the north shore of the reservoir, then continue east along a rough dirt road for approximately 4.2 miles to Mineral Basin and the trailhead.

High-clearance vehicles are recommended for this drive, which crosses a very narrow section of road with steep drop-offs to the river. Beyond the narrow stretch, the valley opens into Mineral Basin/Dutchman Flat. No signs mark the trail. Look for a wooden fence on the right side of the road, near the river, with a few vehicle parking spaces. The trail, a jeep road, lies across the American Fork River (on the right/south), and heads southeast.

Forest Lake

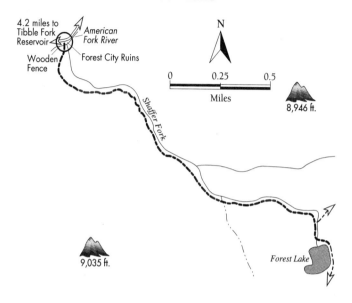

Caution: Exercise extreme care when driving to the trailhead. Narrow sections of the dirt access road can be extremely dangerous when there is opposing traffic.

Key points:
0.2 The main road turns north.
0.4 Pass a large sink hole.
1.2 Cross a small stream.
1.7 Take a right turn to the lake.
1.9 Arrive at Forest Lake.

The hike: If you enjoy abundant wildflowers and serene views, the hike to Forest Lake is an excellent choice. During mid-summer, bluebells are in full bloom and the picturesque lake, standing quietly as a holding basin for snowmelt, is a great place for picnicking, napping, or just listening to the birds.

The trail is actually a very rough jeep road, allowing several family members to hike side by side. Numerous other trail users share this trail including four-wheel-drive and all-terrain vehicles, and horseback riders. Be courteous to other users to make the experience enjoyable for everyone. Stinging nettle grows along the trail and it is advisable to teach the youngsters to avoid their painful leaves.

From the trailhead, you can see remnants of historic Forest City, including an old smelter, charcoal kilns, and areas where homes used to be. You may need to use a little imagination, since most of the buildings have fallen, burnt down, or were destroyed. Careful inspection, however, will help locate leveled areas and remnants of rusting equipment.

Your journey begins after you cool your feet by fording the river. Follow the main jeep trail, which heads in a south-easterly direction and gently climbs the hillside. Numerous side roads and campsites make pleasant picnic sites, though they also might complicate route-finding. Continue south-east until you arrive at a fork in the road at 0.2 miles. Take the left (north) fork, which is the main path heading into the bottom of a narrow little canyon. The trail, in general, is covered with shade, and numerous wildflowers line the path.

After passing a large sinkhole in the road at 0.4 miles, the trail heads southeast again. Proceeding up the canyon, at 1.2 miles the trail becomes somewhat steeper and crosses parts of the Shaffer Fork. There are some loose rocks in the trail and it is advisable to watch your footing as you climb. The shaded hike levels off before reaching a fork near a wooden trail sign at 1.7 miles. Take the right fork, heading south over the brightly lit hill, to the lake at 1.9 miles.

After relaxing and taking in the views, return to trail-head via the same route.

23
SCOUT FALLS

Type of hike: Out-and-back.
Total distance: 3.0 miles.
Elevation gain: 600 feet.
Maps: USGS Timpanogos Cave.
Jurisdiction: Mount Timpanogos Wilderness Area, Uinta National Forest.
Finding the trailhead: Drive 7.4 miles east on Utah 92 from Interstate 15/Exit 287 to the information/fee station at the mouth of American Fork Canyon. Continue east into American Fork Canyon for approximately 4.6 miles past the fee station to where the North Fork/Utah 144 branches to the left (north). At this junction, continue ahead on UT 92 (the South Fork). The road continues past Mutual Dell. The Timpooneke turnoff, heading west, is approximately 8 miles from the fee station (look for the sign). Follow the Timpooneke road to the parking area. Restroom facilities and drinking water are available at the trailhead.

Key points:
0.1 Pass the guard station and continue on right upper trail.
0.6 The trail becomes less shaded.
1.2 Water crosses the trail.
1.4 Continue east at the switchback.
1.5 Arrive at Scout Falls.

Scout Falls

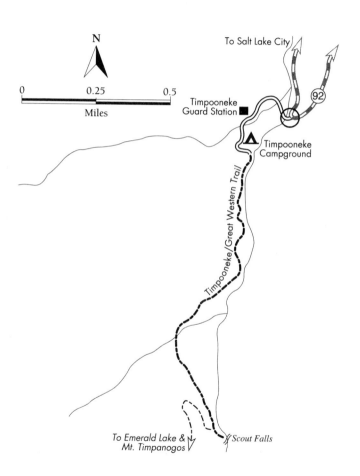

N

| 0 | 0.25 | 0.5 |

Miles

To Salt Lake City

92

Timpooneke
Guard Station

Timpooneke
Campground

Timpooneke/Great Western Trail

To Emerald Lake &
Mt. Timpanogos

Scout Falls

On the east-facing slope, you may view beaver ponds below and columbine along the path. As you climb further, you may admire views of magnificent rock walls capped with pines. These same walls echo with the sounds of the waterfalls.

Groves of aspen appear as the path leads though elderberry and stinging nettle. Caution should be exercised to avoid a painful reminder of the nettles' presence. Mountain ash, catnip, coneflower, and sweet pea can be seen among the aspen. The trail maintains its course to the right of the big meadow below.

The trail emerges from the shade at 0.6 mile, and the sound of water becomes much louder. As you approach the southern end of the valley at 1.2 miles, water crosses the trail at several points, and it can become quite slick. Younger children may require help to cross these small streams. Water-loving vegetation including ferns and bluebells are abundant. Although these tiny waterfalls may quench the heat, your goal is just a few minutes away.

As the main trail turns east and approaches a switchback at 1.4 miles, a less-traveled path continues east to Scout Falls (1.5 miles). Willows are abundant here, along with bluebells, elderberry, and other wildflowers. A few resting areas allow you to enjoy the views before returning to the trailhead by the same route.

Options: You can continue on the Timpooneke/Great Western Trail to Emerald Lake (approximately 5 miles from the falls) or the summit of Mount Timpanogos (approximately 8 miles above the falls).

The hike: Scout Falls completes the first leg of the Timpooneke Trail to the summit of Mount Timpanogos, and is a magnificent sight during the early summer months, when snow melting from above feeds the cascade. Later in the season, the falls become little more than a trickle.

Many families enjoy this hike, which is part of the Great Western Trail, making it a tradition to stop at the refreshing falls before continuing to the summit. Wildflowers adorn the trail, like jewels on a crown, and beyond the falls, some of the most spectacular wildflower displays along the Wasatch Front are available.

This wide, well-designed trail is shaded by aspen, although it can be quite warm during late morning and early afternoon. Early morning and early evening hikes are recommended to avoid heat exhaustion. This route climbs at a steady rate, is well-marked, and easily navigated by most hikers. Wildflowers are abundant and views of deer and moose are not uncommon. A rustic overlook is available near the falls, from which you can enjoy the views of a lush green valley below and feel the refreshing mist of the falls.

From the parking area, head through a meadow full of asters and sweet pea to the guard station, located southwest of the restrooms. Here, you can familiarize yourself with local hazards, learn about wilderness etiquette, and sign the trail register. Horses share this trail and hikers should avoid spooking them to avoid injury.

Take the right (west) trail at 0.1 mile, and follow the well-defined path south through a meadow surrounded by pines and quaking aspen, The trail climbs steadily through coneflower and cow parsnips.

24
CASCADE SPRINGS
INTERPRETIVE TRAIL

Type of hike: Loop.
Total distance: 0.6 mile.
Elevation gain: 75 feet.
Maps: USGS Aspen Grove.
Jurisdiction: Uinta National Forest.
Finding the trailhead: Drive 7.4 miles east on Utah 92 from Interstate 15/Exit 287 to the information/fee station at the mouth of American Fork Canyon. Continue east into American Fork Canyon for approximately 4.6 miles past the fee station to where the North Fork branches to the left (north). At this junction, continue ahead on UT 92 (the South Fork). The road continues past Mutual Dell and the Timpooneke turnoff. Stay east on UT 92 and wind over the summit. Cascade Springs Road branches to the east at 10.9 miles, just as the road begins down the Provo Canyon side. Turn onto Cascade Springs Road and head east until you see the Cascade Springs turnoff into the parking area (17.9 miles).

Key points:
0.1 Trails converge before crossing the bridge.
0.2 Climb stairs to the second loop.
0.3 Begin the Springs Loop.
0.6 Return to the trailhead.

Cascade Springs Interpretive Trail

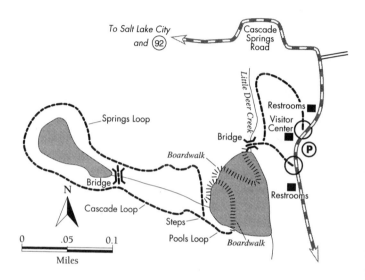

The hike: A winding maze of boardwalks and paths wander the shaded area known as Cascade Springs, with interpretive signs that offer a greater understanding of the water cycle. Trout cautiously rest in the cold pools, waiting for unsuspecting insects. Although this path can be covered in a matter of minutes, this area can be best enjoyed if you leisurely watch the fish, read the signs, and take the time to absorb the beauty that makes this area unique.

Over 7,000,000 gallons of water emerge from the ground in this area, cascading over travertine ledges, splashing into dark pools, and racing into Provo Deer Creek. Numerous benches have been provided along the trails for resting and the paths have been improved to provide access to people with disabilities.

Numerous route options are available in this area, allowing you to determine which path best meets your needs. Three major loops offer different perspectives and cater to different ability levels. Wheelchair and stroller access is only available on the cooler Pools Loop.

Observe the maps near the parking area, which detail the routes around the springs. Wheelchairs may best access the area by taking the right (north) trail, making a gentle decent. Others may take the steeper route to the left, near the gazebo. Both trails converge below and continue south, along the creek. Cross the bridge at 0.1 mile and enter the boardwalk area. Vegetation is lush here and the sound of running water quiets the soul.

Wander through the maze of boardwalks and read the interpretive signs as you look for wildlife. You may spot trout splashing in the pools, see a hummingbird, or hear the buzz of a dragonfly. Fishing is not permitted at the springs.

Flowers are abundant, and you can expect to find wild rose, snowberry, showy daisy, columbine, monkshood, watercress, sagebrush and serviceberry.

At the southwestern part of the boardwalk, a trail climbs several steps at 0.2 mile and heads west to the Cascades Loop and the Springs Loop. These sections are not wheelchair accessible, and may be difficult for some, but it is quiet and beautiful, and offers additional information to the visitor. As you travel west, a bridge crosses the waters to the right (north) to complete the Cascades Loop. Continuing west (straight ahead) at 0.3 mile takes you onto the Springs Loop. As you return to the north side of the bridge, you may cross it to return down the path you came up on, or you may complete the northern section of the Cascades Loop, heading east, to the boardwalk below.

Upon reaching the boardwalk again, proceed to the parking area at your leisure, or stop to learn more about the area at the visitor center at 0.6 mile.

About the Author

Brian Brinkerhoff is a lifetime Utah resident and enjoys the beautiful mountain splendor of the area. He enjoys a wide range of outdoor related activities from hunting, fishing, and hiking to boating, camping, and skiing. He is employed as an outdoor correspondent for the Newtah News Group, with articles covering northern Utah County published in *New Utah!* He also hosts Backcountry Utah, an outdoor radio program, broadcasting on AM-630 KTKK and has served on the board of directors of the Great Western Trail Association.